Mensa®
Book

Challenging Word Search Puzzles
for kids

Mark Danna

STERLING

New York / London

www.sterlingpublishing.com/kids

For everyone who's up for a good challenge

2 4 6 8 10 9 7 5 3 1

Published by Sterling Publishing Co., Inc.
387 Park Avenue South, New York, NY 10016
© 2008 by Mark Danna
Distributed in Canada by Sterling Publishing
C/o Canadian Manda Group, 165 Dufferin Street
Toronto, Ontario, Canada M6K 3H6
Distributed in the United Kingdom by GMC Distribution Services
Castle Place, 166 High Street, Lewes, East Sussex, England BN7 1XU
Distributed in Australia by Capricorn Link (Australia) Pty. Ltd.
P.O. Box 704, Windsor, NSW 2756, Australia

Sterling ISBN 978-1-4027-4675-8

For information about custom editions, special sales, premium and
corporate purchases, please contact Sterling Special Sales
Department at 800-805-5489 or specialsales@sterlingpublishing.com.

Contents

Introduction

Playful shapes, terrific themes, teasing twists, hidden messages, and a whole lot more . . . that's what you get when you tackle these *Challenging Word Search Puzzles for Kids.*

What's special about this book? It's by puzzle pro Mark Danna, America's foremost creator of picture-shaped word searches. This is his fourteenth word search book for Sterling.

Grids. About half of the puzzle grids in this book are in the standard rectangular format. In the other half, the grid letters combine to form a picture: a penguin, a rocket ship, a sea serpent, a wedding cake, and a volcano, to name just a few. In every case, the shape is geared to the puzzle's theme, and the fun shapes definitely add to the enjoyment.

Themes. There are 51 puzzles, each with a different theme. Themes range from national flags to weird collections to Lewis and Clark to movies with aliens. With so many fresh ideas, this book will keep you entertained for weeks.

Twists. Besides great shapes and themes, we've added some twists. In the three rebus puzzles, a little picture represents a set of letters. For example, in "Auto Focus" every word or phrase in the word list contains the letters C-A-R in consecutive order. When these words appear in the grid, the letters C-A-R show up as a little 🚗 . So the word SCARECROW in the word list would appear as S 🚗 ECROW in the grid. An added challenge? You bet! In other rebuses, instead of searching for cars, you'll be looking for little pens and pieces of A-R-T.

In another twist, some of the grids have no word list: It's up to you to build it! You do that by using the clues given. For example, in "Simply Super," you need to come up with the second part of a compound word or phrase in which both parts start with the letter S. So if you're given the clue SUN_ _ _ _ _ _ (Lotion to protect you from betting burned at the beach), you'd fill in the blanks with SCREEN. Then you'd search for SCREEN in the grid. In "Same and Different," you'll figure out words that are spelled the same but have very different meanings. In "Triple Play," you'll identify what sets of initials like NFL stand for. And in "Heads or Tails" you'll discover words that are linked at their starting and ending letters.

You'll also find a gimmick in "Do You Read Me?" but we wouldn't want to spoil the surprise here.

Hidden Messages. A big bonus is: *Every puzzle has a hidden message!* After you circle all the words and phrases in the grid, read all the uncircled letters from left to right and top to bottom to spell out a fascinating fact, a funny line, a tongue twister, an interesting observation, or more words connected to the theme. The leftover letters will be in order, but you'll need to determine where to break them up into words and where to add punctuation. This puzzle-within-a-puzzle is truly challenging, adding a level of difficulty not usually associated with word search puzzles. If it proves to be too much of a challenge, that's okay. You can enjoy all of the hidden messages by reading them in the answer section.

How to Solve. Finding the hidden messages may be tough, but learning to solve word searches is easy. If you know how to do them, jump right in. If you don't know how, keep on reading and we'll tell you everything you need to know.

The Basics. A word search is a game of hide-and-seek: we hide the words, you go seek them. Each puzzle has two main parts: a grid and a word list. The grid is a jumble of letters that hide all the words and phrases in the word list. In the grid, words always run in a straight line—horizontally, vertically, or diagonally. Horizontal words go straight across normally or backward. Vertical words go straight down or straight up. Diagonal words slant from left to right or right to left and go either upward or downward along the angle. That means that words can go in eight possible directions—along the lines of a plus sign (+) or a multiplication sign (X).

Getting Started. Some people look for across words first. Others begin with the long words or ones with less common letters like J, Q, X, and Z. Still others start at the top of the list and work their way in order straight down to the bottom. Try a few ways and see what works best for you.

Marking the Words. Loop them, draw a straight line through them, or circle each individual letter. Whichever way you choose, cross the words off the word list as you find them in the grid so as to avoid confusion. Also, be sure to be neat. Neatness will help when you're looking for all the letters that make up the hidden message.

Ignore Punctuation. When you look for words and phrases in the grid, ignore all punctuation and spacing in the word list. For example, the phrase "THAT DEPENDS…" in the word list would appear in the grid, in some direction, as THATDEPENDS. Also, ignore all words in brackets like [THE] and [A]. These have been added at times to make certain word list items more understandable, but these bracketed words will not appear in the grid.

It All Connects. In all of Danna's books, each word in a grid shares at least one letter in common with another word, and all the words in a grid interconnect. It's much harder and more time-consuming to make a puzzle this way—which is why most puzzlemakers don't. We do it because we believe it adds elegance to the construction.

Difficulty Levels. The rebus puzzles and the ones with missing word lists are tougher, but the rest of the puzzles are about the same level of difficulty—that is, challenging but not mind-crushing. In all but five puzzles, the number of items in a word list ranges from 16 to 24—not too long but not too short. Feel free to jump around and solve the puzzles in any order you like.

Some Final Tips. Many puzzle titles are "punny" and may mislead you at first as to what the theme is. Several of the hidden messages contain facts, historical and otherwise, that may truly surprise you. And finally, as you're now set to begin, we hope you'll thoroughly enjoy the challenge of these puzzles—right from the "Opening Bell" to the "Closing Notice."

1. OPENING BELL

Shaped like a bell, this first grid quite appropriately contains words and phrases associated with the start of something. For example, a bell could mean the start of class, the beginning of a horse race, or the opening of the New York Stock Exchange. The hidden message offers a suggestion on how to get off to a good start.

```
                P
                R
                E
          N  N  S  E  E
       V  T  E  S  L  R  S
    C  E  T  I  S  F  N  G  A
    R  H  R  R  T  F  I  N  F
    T  N  A  A  A  U  E  A  F
    U  D  A  P  R  H  V  B  O
 S  E  E  D  Y  T  S  I  G  K  B
 R  O  L  L  T  H  E  D  I  C  E
 W  I  O  I  T  L  T  R  B  I  L
 H  G  S  R  H  E  L  L  O  K  L
O  O  F  I  R  S  T  S  C  E  N  E  U
N  T  B  A  D  A  T  A  R  I  S  E  R
                E
             E  R  D
             A  A  M
```

ARISE	DIVE IN	LOG ON
BELL	ENTER	PRESS "START"
BIG BANG	FIRST SCENE	ROLL THE DICE
BIRTH	HELLO	SEED
CHAPTER ONE	KICKOFF	SHUFFLE
DEAR SIR	[THE] LETTER A	SUNRISE

2. COMING UP

Shaped like an up arrow, this grid contains the names of shapes coming up in the puzzles ahead. The hidden message gives you a preview of two more shapes.

```
                  A
               H  P  L
            I  N  C  G  I
         V  B  O  T  T  L  E
      P  O  O  N  G  N  I  P  N
   A  D  L  O  C  K  E  D  W  L  E
T  R  A  C  G  N  I  P  P  O  H  S  A
      A  E  M  A  R  F  E
      N  S  T  R  E  E  L
      O  A  N  D  S  C  E
      A  V  S  T  A  M  P
      R  O  C  K  E  T  H
      F  A  E  C  S  E  A
      P  E  N  G  U  I  N
      S  K  I  B  O  O  T
```

ALIEN	PENGUIN	STAMP
BOTTLE	ROCKET	TREE
CAKE	SEA SERPENT	VASE
ELEPHANT	SHOPPING CART	VOLCANO
FRAME	SKI BOOT	WITCH
LOCK		

3. BIRTH OF A NATION

This grid contains words associated with the American Revolutionary War. The bird chosen to be a national symbol was the bald eagle, but Benjamin Franklin wasn't so keen about it. He said the bird was too lazy to fish and stole its meals from other animals who had done the hard work. The hidden message tells what Franklin felt was a better choice.

```
M  O  M  I  N  U  T  E  M  E  N
S  Y  S  S  E  R  G  N  O  C  B
T  E  M  R  L  E  I  R  S  U  O
A  G  E  R  L  T  I  S  N  E  S
O  R  P  E  A  O  I  K  O  D  T
C  O  L  O  N  I  E  S  N  I  O
D  F  C  T  A  R  G  A  N  R  N
E  Y  B  L  H  T  R  E  A  T  Y
R  E  E  I  T  A  O  H  C  H  T
E  L  L  S  E  P  E  R  A  G  R
I  L  D  I  S  T  G  H  Y  I  A
W  A  S  H  I  N  G  T  O  N  P
E  V  T  F  R  A  N  C  E  D  A
U  R  B  R  I  T  I  S  H  I  E
K  E  Y  S  T  E  K  S  U  M  T
```

ARMY	ETHAN ALLEN	REDCOATS
BOSTON	FRANCE	TEA PARTY
BRITISH	KING GEORGE III	TORY
BUNKER HILL	MIDNIGHT RIDE	TREATY
CANNONS	MINUTEMEN	VALLEY FORGE
COLONIES	MUSKETS	WASHINGTON
CONGRESS	PATRIOT	

4. TAKE YOUR PICK

This lock-shaped grid contains things that you pick, including NITS, as in the word "nitpick." Nowadays, nitpick means to criticize by picking out small, minor details, but the hidden message is a definition of what nitpick originally meant, which is kind of icky.

```
            R  N  E
         M  O     O  V
      M  S           E  P
      E                 P
      A                 C
      T                 K
      F  D  M  T  E  S  E
   A  R  G  U  M  E  N  T  I
   N  A  O  Y  S  L  S  I  S  I  I
C  C  E  M  E  H  F  O  A  G  G  N  S
G  U  I  T  A  R  S  T  R  I  N  G  S
F  R  O  H  I  O  F  E  B  M  S  F  I
H  T  E  E  T  O  B  I  O  M  N  L  D
E  O  N  B  L  M  N  V  G  E  O  O  E
B  D  S  O  U  S  H  O  A  H  T  W  S
S  A  C  N  T  E  A  M  M  A  T  E  S
I  K  C  E  G  E  L  L  O  C  O  R  R
   R  O  S  S  E  C  C  U  S  C  S
```

ARGUMENT	FRIENDS	NOSE
[SOMEBODY'S]	GUITAR STRINGS	NUMBER
BRAINS	LOCK	POCKETS
CARD	MEAT FROM THE	SCAB
COLLEGE	BONES	SIDES
COTTON	MOVIE TO SEE	SUCCESSOR
FIGHT	MUSHROOMS	TEAMMATES
FLOWERS	NITS	TEETH

5. THE PENGUIN

Shaped like a penguin, this grid contains words about that bird. The hidden message defines "toboggan," which is something some penguins do.

```
            E  E  T
      W  A  D  D  L  E  S
            O  O  D  T
            P  F  D
         R  P  H  A  L  U  V
      P  A  R  T  S  N  I  H  C
   E  B  D  O  U  L  H  O  P  U  P
   Y  I  B  T  O  Y  B  E  L  P  L
Y  V  L  S  E  S  R  E  H  T  A  E  F
   E  L  F  C  L  O  I  D  O  I     R
S  N  M  A  T  E  C  G  R  B  M     A  S
C     O  O  T  N  E  G  O  O  A        R
      O  S  H  S  A  I  R  G  R
      C  N  E  E  N  C  E  G  C
      T  E  E  F  Y  P  P  A  H
      O  G  S  I  R  M  N
      G  S  T  S  E
      N  O        H  W
```

BILL	FLIPPERS	NEST
CAN'T FLY	GENTOO	OCEAN
CHINSTRAP	*HAPPY FEET*	PROTECT THE EGG
DIVES	HOP UP	SOUTH POLE
EMPEROR	HUDDLE	TOBOGGAN
FEATHERS	MARCH	WADDLES
FISH	MATE	

6. PICK A NUMBER

This grid contains phrases that each have at least two digits. The hidden message names three classic books — all made into movies — that also have at least two digits in their titles.

```
T D 1 9 S W E E T 1 6
C N O I S I V 0 2 0 2
A E 8 A 4 C 1 5 7 1 A
T W 0 T 3 G C 6 R D H
N S 2 1 N 6 2 T A A F
O A A A C H 0 I P L R
C T H P 1 A E M N M A
1 1 G H 7 E P I I A G
2 1 G U N S A L U T E
3 1 1 9 L A I D T I N
6 0 M I N U T E S A T
4 5 7 5 Z N I E H N 0
0 5 0 5 T I L P S S 0
T O P 1 0 L I S T 1 7
```

101 DALMATIANS	DO A 360	PAR 72
20/20 VISION	HANG 10	PG-13
21-GUN SALUTE	HEINZ 57	SPEED LIMIT 65
3-2-1 CONTACT	NC-17	SPLIT 50-50
60 MINUTES	NEWS AT 11	SWEET 16
AGENT 007	PAC-10	TOP 10 LIST
DIAL 911		

7. ALIEN INVASION

Shaped like a space alien's head, this grid contains words and phrases from movies and reports about alien sightings. Just imagine how shocked our world would be if a space alien's first spoken words to us were those found in the hidden message!

```
            Y  X  A  L  A  G
         I  W  A  R  P  D  R  I  V  E
      T  N  H  I  N  L  L  E  W  S  O  R
   W  A  R  O  F  T  H  E  W  O  R  L  D  S
A  H  O  S  T  I  L  E  T  E  N  A  L  P  C  P
L  T        K  W  S  C  E  A  R  E        I  O
I  L  T        S  R  A  M  L  O        S  F  D
E  T  C  A        A  P  V  O        N  Y  I  S
N  O  R  E  C  U  A  S  G  N  I  Y  L  F  R  U
   R  T  E  S  K  B  R  L  E  I  L  U  E  S
      O  E  M  O  H  E  N  O  H  P  T  E
      H  M  O  S  F  T  A  W  N  N  L  T
         U  O  P  U  G  M  U  I
            L  T  O  E  O  G
            T  A  T  C  H  Y
            O  K  N  T  K  A
            V  E  S  S  E  R
            N  N  U  S
```

ALIEN	HOSTILE	ROMULANS
ARE WE ALONE?	INVASION	ROSWELL
ATTACK	LIGHTS	SCI-FI
BEAM	MARS	SPOCK
ENCOUNTERS	OUTER SPACE	TAKEN
"E.T. PHONE HOME"	PLANET	UFOS
FLYING SAUCER	PODS	*WAR OF THE WORLDS*
GALAXY	RAY GUN	WARP DRIVE

8. THIS IS *JEOPARDY!*

This grid contains words and phrases associated with the TV game show *Jeopardy!* The hidden message answers this: What two game shows — each running on TV for more than 40 years — were ranked by *TV Guide* as #2 and #1 of the 50 Best Game Shows of All Time? (Be sure your answer is phrased in the form of a question.)

```
W  H  H  A  N  D  S  H  A  K  E
A  C  S  H  O  W  F  T  I  I  T
A  O  T  R  I  V  I  A  S  D  H
N  N  J  E  T  R  N  O  R  S  I
S  T  P  A  S  O  A  R  E  W  R
W  E  R  C  E  U  L  C  Z  E  T
E  S  D  Y  U  N  J  A  Z  E  Y
R  T  O  N  Q  D  E  D  U  K  S
D  A  I  L  Y  D  O  U  B  L  E
T  N  D  N  O  I  P  M  A  H  C
C  T  U  R  E  G  A  W  X  H  O
C  A  T  E  G  O  R  I  E  S  N
E  P  S  R  A  I  D  C  L  E  D
I  S  R  H  M  I  Y  G  A  H  S
T  H  E  M  E  M  U  S  I  C  T
```

ALEX	CONTESTANT	ROUND
ANSWER	DAILY DOUBLE	SHOW
BUZZER	FINAL JEOPARDY	STUDIO
CASH	GAME	THEME MUSIC
CATEGORIES	HANDSHAKE	THIRTY SECONDS
CHAMPION	KIDS WEEK	TRIVIA
CLUE CREW	QUESTION	WAGER

9. AUTO FOCUS

Each item in this word list contains the letters C-A-R in consecutive order. When these letters appear in the grid, they have been replaced by a 🚗. So, for example, CARGO SHIP would appear as 🚗GOSHIP. Now don't let this S🚗E you! The hidden message is a silly sentence in which we've parked a few more 🚗s.

```
🚗 U O B I 🚗 L W A 🚗 Y
🚗 B O N D I O X I D E
E X 🚗 I F O U L R L R
🚗 Y N A D 🚗 S 🚗 C E 🚗
R A I 🚗 F I D E R D M
L A V P S E 🚗 Y A D I
🚗 E O A P 🚗 R T F O J
R N R L O T E O T M F
M L E T S O T C 🚗 A A
🚗 E 🚗 U T O S O R 🚗 O
R E I N 🚗 N A T I O N
O H N N D E M S E N W
T W T E O 🚗 S A R I C
S T E L 🚗 S S S I M A
S 🚗 N I V A L E M A 🚗
```

AIRCRAFT CARRIER	CARNIVAL	MACARONI
BOXCAR	CARNIVORE	MASTERCARD
CARAFE	CARPAL TUNNEL	MISS SCARLET
CARAMEL	CARROTS	POSTCARD
CARBON DIOXIDE	CARTOON	REINCARNATION
CARDINAL	CARTWHEEL	SCARCE
CARESS	DAY CARE	SCARECROW
CARIBOU	JIM CARREY	WOODCARVER

10. POP CULTURE

Shaped like a two-liter bottle of soda pop, this grid contains the names of soft drinks and soft drink companies. A certain famous soft drink was first served at a soda fountain in a Texas drug store. The owner was one Wade Morrison, who named the drink for a friend. Read the hidden message to find out who it was. You should then be able to figure out what the soda is called.

```
              F  C  A
              D  A  O
           D  R  O  N  K
        C  S  P  R  I  T  E
        W  T  E  S  P  O  A
     S  E  P  P  E  W  H  C  S
     S  D  R  P  R  N  E  H  I
     L  N  S  E  I  E  N  S  B
     I  I  A  R  H  L  M  U  O
     C  A  N  A  D  A  D  R  Y
     E  T  V  J  E  R  E  C  L
     P  N  E  O  D  E  C  E  A
     H  U  R  L  B  G  A  G  N
     A  O  N  T  R  N  T  N  S
     L  M  O  E  E  I  S  A  S
     T  O  R  S  V  G  A  R  P
     R  E  S  D  P  E  H  O  P
        E  B  A  R  Q  S  R
        W  D  N  A  A
```

A AND W	GINGER ALE	ROOT BEER
BARQ'S	HIRES	SCHWEPPES
BOYLAN'S	JOLT	SEVEN-UP
CANADA DRY	MOUNTAIN DEW	SHASTA
COKE	NEHI	SLICE
DAD'S	ORANGE CRUSH	SPRITE
DR PEPPER	PEPSI	VERNOR'S
FANTA		

11. HITS POSSIBLE

Shaped like a Ping-Pong paddle, this grid contains things you hit a ball with. These things come from sports and games such as baseball, golf, soccer, football, croquet, squash, field hockey, volleyball, and Ping-Pong. The hidden message tells what some peasants in the Middle Ages did for entertainment.

```
            P L P A D Y
          H E E L D D A P
        E D T A F H A N E D
      D B S D R I V E R A H L
      A N O T H E R B A L L L
      I T A B L L A B E S A B
      T G P H A D C M E A G A
      S Q U A S H R A C K E T
      I I T N P O O L C U E I
      F S T T A C Q C H F R A
        P E E N K U W O O D
          R E L E E O N W
            A Y T L
              S M
              T A
              I L
              C L
              K E
              L T
```

ANOTHER BALL	FOOT	KNEE
BASEBALL BAT	HAND	PADDLE
CROQUET MALLET	HEAD	POOL CUE
DRIVER	HEEL	PUTTER
FIELD HOCKEY STICK	INSTEP	SQUASH RACKET
FIST	IRON	WOOD

12. SIMPLY SUPER

Shaped like a sea serpent, this grid contains words that complete a compound word or phrase in which both parts start with the letter S. For example, compound words can be two-syllable words such as SWEEPSTAKES, or hyphenated such as SIX-SHOOTER. Phrases can be something like SOCIAL STUDIES or STAFF SERGEANT. It's up to you to create the word list by using the clues on the next page. The number of blanks tell you the number of letters in the word. To help you, the hidden words are in alphabetical order. If you're doing just SO-SO or are at a complete STANDSTILL, you can turn to the complete word list on page 66. The hidden message is a simple sentence of three more SS words.

```
            S   E   R   V   I   C   E
          T   S   E   ●   S   V   S   E   N
        N   O   M   I   S   H   U   T   T   L   E   T
      Y   R   S   I       R   P   X   A   S   O
      Y               N   E   E   R   C   S   P
            H   I   O   R   V   R   S   K   T   E
      S   I   C   K       I   S   L   U   T
      O   P   S           N   S   H   I   N   E
                          T   M   E   T   S   Y   S
                      R   E   K   A   H   S   E
                    S   O   N   G   O   U   R   S
                  S   T   T   D   V   D   P
                D   N   O   C   E   S   E
              E   H   R   L   N   N   E   S   A
              S   W   M   S   T   R   O   K   E   E   D
```

1. SUN_ _ _ _ _ _   Lotion to protect you from getting burned at the beach

2. SPLIT-_ _ _ _ _ _   Very small unit of time

3. SEA _ _ _ _ _ _ _   Mythical beast that tormented sailors

4. SELF-_ _ _ _ _ _ _   Do-it-yourself pumping at a gas station

5. SALT _ _ _ _ _ _   Container you use to season your food

6. SHOE _ _ _ _ _   Polished finish on your footwear

7. SNAP_ _ _ _   Photo

8. SNOW _ _ _ _ _ _   Tool for clearing your driveway in winter

9. SPACE _ _ _ _ _ _ _   Astronauts' vehicle

10. SEA_ _ _ _   How you might feel being tossed on the ocean

11. STERLING _ _ _ _ _ _   High-quality metal in jewelry

12. SIMPLE _ _ _ _ _   Character who met a pieman

13. SHEEP_ _ _ _   A woolly animal's hide

14. SKI _ _ _ _ _   Mountain descent for winter recreation

15. SWAN _ _ _ _   Final public appearance, or a dying bird's melody

16. SMOKE_ _ _ _ _   Chimney at a factory

17. SHOOTING _ _ _ _   Meteor streaking across the night sky

18. SAND_ _ _ _ _   Bad, windy weather in the desert

19. SCARY _ _ _ _ _   Ghostly tale

20. SIDE_ _ _ _ _ _   Technique used in a pool

21. SOAP_ _ _ _   Froth in bath water

22. SWIM_ _ _ _   Bikini, for example

23. SCHOOL _ _ _ _ _ _ _ _ _ _ _ _ _ _   One who oversees principals and teachers

24. SOLAR _ _ _ _ _ _   Our sun and planets all together

13. ISLE OF TWOPLAY

This grid contains the names of islands or island countries. The hidden message explains something unusual about the grid.

```
L  I  D  K  G  U  A  M  J  E  M
E  S  N  S  C  E  P  A  A  T  O
A  P  A  R  R  P  A  A  R  D
S  U  L  I  T  A  E  I  E  A  G
T  E  A  L  N  I  W  T  S  C  N
E  R  E  A  L  A  A  N  E  S  I
R  T  Z  N  N  D  S  B  N  A  K
I  O  W  K  O  N  A  E  H  G  D
S  R  E  A  D  H  O  A  F  A  E
L  I  N  T  A  N  W  H  F  D  T
A  C  E  M  W  A  A  I  O  A  I
N  O  A  R  I  D  J  L  S  M  N
D  S  C  I  O  I  N  N  E  E  U
I  N  D  O  N  E  S  I  A  C  C
A  U  S  T  R  A  L  I  A  T  I
```

AUSTRALIA	HAWAII	NEW ZEALAND
BAHAMAS	ICELAND	PUERTO RICO
CRETE	INDONESIA	SRI LANKA
EASTER ISLAND	JAPAN	TAIWAN
FIJI	MADAGASCAR	UNITED KINGDOM
GUAM		

14. LEWIS AND CLARK

This grid contains words relating to the great Lewis and Clark expedition. A Scotsman named Alexander Mackenzie also made an historic crossing of the North American continent. The hidden message reveals a fact that is surprising to most Americans about Mackenzie in relation to Lewis and Clark.

```
H  S  P  R  O  C  E  C  G  E  D
I  N  S  E  O  N  A  C  R  R  D
N  A  I  V  S  M  T  E  E  O  A
O  I  F  I  P  I  G  U  A  L  L
R  D  L  R  T  A  W  E  T  P  A
T  N  O  I  T  I  D  E  P  X  E
H  I  J  R  G  N  J  Y  L  E  W
W  J  O  U  R  N  E  Y  A  S  A
E  P  U  O  I  E  F  S  I  E  G
S  A  R  S  Z  R  F  L  N  I  A
T  P  N  S  Z  S  E  L  S  K  C
E  A  A  I  L  K  R  A  L  C  A
R  L  L  M  Y  I  S  F  E  O  S
B  U  F  F  A  L  O  H  E  R  D
F  O  R  T  M  A  N  D  O  N  R
```

BUFFALO HERD	FORT MANDON	LEWIS
CAMP	GREAT PLAINS	MAPS
CANOES	GRIZZLY	MISSOURI RIVER
CLARK	INDIANS	NORTHWEST
CORPS	JEFFERSON	PORTAGE
EXPEDITION	JOURNAL	ROCKIES
EXPLORE	JOURNEY	SACAGAWEA
FALLS		

15. "CUT!"

Shaped like a wedding cake, this grid contains things you cut. The hidden message answers this question: In making paper dolls, what can happen if you're not careful when you cut the paper?

```
            B  U  D  G  E  T  Y
            C  O  R  N  E  R  S
            C  H  E  E  S  E  O
            T           E
            O           L
   S  S  A  L  C  R  N  I  A  R  G
   C  H  E  C  K  E  U  M  M  E  A
   Y  S  S  A  R  G  G  B  E  N  D
   E  K  A  C  G  N  I  D  D  E  W
      T        I        C
      A        F        S
P  S  U  P  P  L  Y  L  I  N  E  S  A
H  C  T  O  N  S  A  N  D  W  I  C  H
T  A  P  E  N  I  G  N  E  P  V  E  R
P  R  I  C  E  S  N  E  S  N  O  N  C
   C  A  R  D  D  E  C  K  U  M  T
```

BUDGET	[THE] ENGINE	NOTCH
CARD DECK	FINGER	PRICES
[A] CHECK	GRAIN	SANDWICH
CHEESE	GRASS	SUPPLY LINES
CLASS	HAIR	TAPE
CLOTH	MOVIE SCENE	TREE LIMB
CORNERS	[THE] NONSENSE	WEDDING CAKE
[A] DEAL		

16. A HERD OF ANIMALS

This elephant-shaped grid contains the names of 13 animals and the names of their groups. For example, a group of elephants is a herd, so the list contains a HERD of ELEPHANTS. Don't look for the "of" in the grid. The animals and group names appear separately, so there are 26 words for you to circle. The hidden message names two more types of animals and their group names, which might surprise you.

```
                                                    A  R
                                                    L
                                  M  N               I
             S  P  A  C  K        L  E  A  P         O
          Y  T  M  R  A  W  S     X  L  O  F         N
       F     S  L  F  I  S  H  E  O  L  O  O  H  C  S
       R     U  E  O  E  D  G  U  I  S  H  K  S  A
       M     C  O  N  G  R  E  G  A  T  I  O  N
             O  P  B  N  U  A  A  O  N  S        O
             L  A  S  U  T  B  L  O  A  T        T
          H  O  R  D  O  O  S  P  F  H
          T  A  D  R  L  A  O  E  H  P
          E     S  A     D  P     V  E
       B  A     E  Z     S  P     T  L  R
       I  M     E  I     G  I     E  O  D
       E        B  L     R  H     S  W
```

BLOAT of HIPPOS
CONGREGATION of ALLIGATORS
HERD of ELEPHANTS
KNOT of TOADS

LEAP of LEOPARDS
LOUNGE of LIZARDS
PACK of WOLVES
PLAGUE of LOCUSTS
PRIDE of LIONS

SCHOOL of FISH
SLOTH of BEARS
SWARM of BEES
TEAM of OXEN

17. APT ANAGRAMS

An anagram is a word or phrase spelled by rearranging the letters of another word or phrase. For example, rearrange COAT and you get TACO. Pretty simple. But the anagrams in this puzzle go further: You not only get a new word or phrase, but also an appropriate definition or a surprising new word. For instance, the phrase ELEVEN PLUS TWO is an anagram of TWELVE PLUS ONE! Pretty amazing! The word list is arranged in anagram pairs, and both parts of the anagram pair are hidden in the grid. When you're done, the hidden message will spell out two more anagram pairs with nifty definitions.

```
A  T  H  I  B  T  I  D  E  R  C  D  A  B  S
S  T  A  T  U  E  O  F  L  I  B  E  R  T  Y
T  E  A  L  I  V  E  S  E  R  E  N  Q  F  U
R  T  A  O  L  F  A  L  V  S  I  A  T  O  D
O  N  A  M  T  N  A  G  E  L  E  M  H  L  I
N  S  R  O  T  C  A  E  N  A  R  E  D  A  R
O  S  E  N  O  S  U  L  P  E  V  L  E  W  T
M  P  E  P  S  I  C  O  L  A  A  T  B  L  Y
E  B  I  I  T  E  N  O  U  F  O  N  I  D  R
R  A  V  L  A  P  O  C  S  I  P  E  T  E  O
R  L  A  D  Y  B  U  G  T  T  M  G  C  I  O
E  D  S  E  F  Q  U  A  W  L  A  A  A  R  M
S  G  D  O  R  M  I  T  O  R  Y  R  R  R  L
I  U  F  E  E  O  N  R  E  R  I  M  D  A  M
A  Y  R  R  E  R  A  T  S  N  O  O  M  M  S
```

ACTORS = COSTAR
ADMIRER = MARRIED
ASTRONOMER = MOON STARER
DEBIT CARD = BAD CREDIT
DORMITORY = DIRTY ROOM
ELEVEN PLUS TWO = TWELVE PLUS ONE

ELVIS = LIVES
FLOAT = ALOFT
LADYBUG = BALD GUY
PEPSI-COLA = EPISCOPAL
A GENTLEMAN = ELEGANT MAN
STATUE OF LIBERTY = BUILT TO STAY FREE

18. AT THE SUPERMARKET

Shaped like a shopping cart, this grid contains things commonly found at a supermarket other than food. The hidden message seems to be the rule at any supermarket and it answers this question: How can you tell which is the shortest line to stand in?

```
                                              I   B   T
    E   T   A   R   C   F   R   E   E   Z   E   R   A   D
    S   T   C   E   M   R   A   C   K   S   H   K   E   E
        C   O   N   V   E   Y   O   R   B   E   L   T
        U   U   N   E   S   A   C   Y   R   I   A   D
        L   P   A   I   H   N   T   Y   E   Y   O   U
            O   C   R   D   D   I   S   P   L   A   Y
            N   S   S   A   S   E   V   L   E   H   S
            K   C   A   T   S   E   L   S   I   A
                E   R   E   H   C   T   U   B   C
                                            E
        N   C   A   S   H   R   E   G   I   S   T   E   R
            A   O                   T   G
        E   N   I   L               T   R   A   C
            S   I                   N   B
```

AISLES	COUPON	LINE
BAGS	CRATE	MEAT SLICER
BAKERY	DAIRY CASE	RACKS
BUTCHER	DELI	SCANNER
CANS	DISPLAY	SHELVES
CART	FREEZER	STACK
CASH REGISTER	FRESH DATE	UPC'S
CONVEYOR BELT		

19. SNOW FUN

Shaped like a ski boot, this grid contains words and phrases associated with snow skiing. The hidden message answers this riddle: What's a good way to describe a boy who spent all day skiing but mostly did it while sliding down on his rear?

```
      H  T        E  G
      D  I  T  B  A  R
   R  O  P  E  T  O  W
   E  W  S  E  R  M  S
   C  N  S  N  O  W
S  A  H  K  L  S  I
T  R  I  A  E  E
O  D  L  B  I  R
O  S  L  I  A  R  T
B  U  N  N  Y  S  L  O  P  E
F  E  G  D  O  L  C  I  O  R  S
H  L  O  I  U  L  L  A  F  R  K
M  O  U  N  T  A  I  N  S  T  I
S  O  P  N  G        E  N  T  S  D
```

BINDING	GATES	SKIS
BOOTS	LODGE	SLALOM
BUNNY SLOPE	MOUNTAIN	SNOW
CAST	POLE	T-BAR
CHAIRLIFTS	RACE	TIPS
DOWNHILL	RESORT	TRAILS
FALL	ROPE TOW	

20. QUITE A COLLECTION

Shaped like a snow globe, this grid contains things some people collect. In fact, there are world records for the largest collections of each of the items on this list and for the two other unusual collectibles named in the hidden message.

```
            D   N   U   T
        C   I   R   A   C   F   H   K
    E   C   R   S   E   I   B   R   A   B
    E   T   S   A   P   H   T   O   O   T
N   A   V   E   L   F   L   U   F   F   G   S
R   U   B   B   E   R   D   U   C   K   S   S
S   S   T   O   B   O   R   Y   O   T   K   A
S   N   D   L   T   H   S   E   L   O   S   E
    N   A   G   N   T   S   I   O   D   R
    M   I   W   S   E   L   B   R   A   M
        E   O   O   A   C   E   S   U
            N   C   F   N   E   C
        A   S   U   F   R   D   S   A
    C   P   E   N   S   N   O   L   Y   P
C   H   U   R   C   H   P   L   A   T   E   S
```

BARBIES	[LIVE] FROGS	PYLONS
BOOKS	HATS	RUBBER DUCKS
BOTTLE CAPS	LILACS	SAND
CANOES	MARBLES	SNOW GLOBES
CHURCH PLATES	MENUS	[LOST] SOLES
[INTERNATIONAL] COINS	NAVEL FLUFF	TOOTHPASTE
DICE	[BALLPOINT] PENS	TOY ROBOTS
ERASERS		

21. TRIPLE PLAY

One definition of "acronym" is an abbreviation formed from the initial letters. For example, NPR is an acronym of National Public Radio. So many acronyms have entered our everyday language that we don't often stop to think what the initials stand for. But in this puzzle, you'll need to think of them before you find them in the grid. Each of the 13 acronyms below is three-letters long, so you'll need to find 39 words in all. The blanks and starting letters tell you the number of letters in each word. When you're done, the hidden message will give you two more acronyms and their meanings. If you need help with the list, you can find all the words on page 66.

1. NFL
N _ _ _ _ _ _
F _ _ _ _ _ _
L _ _ _ _ _

2. KFC
K _ _ _ _ _ _
  F _ _ _ _
C _ _ _ _ _ _

3. PTA
P _ _ _ _ _
T _ _ _ _ _ _
A _ _ _ _ _ _ _ _ _

4. MVP
M _ _ _
V _ _ _ _ _ _ _
P _ _ _ _ _

5. CIA
C _ _ _ _ _ _
I _ _ _ _ _ _ _ _ _ _
A _ _ _ _ _

6. DVD
D _ _ _ _ _ _
V _ _ _ _
D _ _ _

7. UFO
U _ _ _ _ _ _ _ _ _ _ _
  F _ _ _ _ _
O _ _ _ _ _

8. WWW
W _ _ _ _
W _ _ _
W _ _

9. VIP
V _ _ _
I _ _ _ _ _ _ _ _
P _ _ _ _ _

10. TLC
T _ _ _ _ _
L _ _ _ _ _
C _ _ _

11. CNN
C _ _ _ _
N _ _ _
N _ _ _ _ _ _

12. IRS
I _ _ _ _ _ _ _
R _ _ _ _ _ _
S _ _ _ _ _ _

13. ATM
A _ _ _ _ _ _ _ _ _
  T _ _ _ _ _
M _ _ _ _ _ _

```
A F U Y I I C H I C K E N
G I N T E L L I G E N C E
E C I V R E S S N N F O F
N R D Y F O O T B A L L R
C R E V E N U E O T Y U I
Y E N I H C A M D I S C E
R T I K C N F N O O I D
G E I Y T E V G R N M N A
Y N F A T N I I O A N T S
R D I G I T A L D L N E S
E E E V L R E T L E O R O
V R D L O A P E R S O N C
A A I I G L S A O O O A I
L C W U L A P C W B P L A
U T E L L E R H J U L M T
A U T O M A T E D G A H I
B I N G O O C R U W Y T O
L N E W S T C A B L E L N
E O N E T W O R K U R B D
```

22. OUT TO SEA

This grid contains the names of famous boats and ships — most of them real but a few fictional. The hidden message truly tells how some crewmen of the U.S. whaling ship Essex survived after their ship was sunk by a whale.

```
A  A  I  R  A  M  A  T  N  A  S
W  N  M  A  Y  F  L  O  W  E  R
A  C  I  R  E  M  A  L  I  T  O
N  H  N  N  O  H  F  D  O  K  T
O  G  R  A  S  O  D  I  C  T  I
D  K  C  A  M  I  R  R  E  M  N
I  H  R  E  L  Y  A  O  A  H  O
E  K  T  E  U  M  T  N  M  E  M
S  O  E  S  S  E  X  S  N  Y  I
O  N  H  I  I  E  B  I  I  P  I
P  T  B  R  T  E  A  D  S  P  E
H  I  Y  R  A  M  N  E  E  U  Q
I  K  N  G  N  P  M  S  A  G  T
E  I  L  T  I  T  A  N  I  C  S
Z  E  D  L  A  V  N  O  X  X  E
```

AMERICA	LUSITANIA	OLD IRONSIDES
ARGO	MAINE	PINTA
BISMARCK	MAYFLOWER	POSEIDON
ESSEX	MERRIMACK	QE 11
EXXON VALDEZ	MONITOR	QUEEN MARY
GUPPY	NINA	SANTA MARIA
HMS BEAGLE	NOAH'S ARK	TITANIC
KON-TIKI		

23. VOLCANO!

Shaped like a volcano with a plume of smoke above, this grid contains words associated with volcanoes. The hidden message answers this riddle: Why was the angry boy like a volcano?

```
            A  M  G  A  M
            A  V  A  L  T
               B  S  N
                  E
               V  S  E
            E  R  U  P  T
            C  I  I  A  N
         U  S  N  V  E  A  T
         R  H  G  U  C  M  S
      A  O  S  O  S  R  R  U  E
      H  C  A  F  E  A  O  N  L
   E  O  K  T  F  V  T  D  A  B  P
   N  E  L  O  I  I  E  P  M  O  P
E  M  E  T  H  R  V  R  W  I  H  I  S
O  T  O  S  N  E  L  E  H  T  S  T  M
D  P  V  U  L  C  A  N  O  L  O  G  I  S  T
```

ACTIVE	GASES	RING OF FIRE
CONE	HOT ASH	ROCK
CRATER	LAVA	TSUNAMI
DOME	MAGMA	VENT
DORMANT	MT. ST. HELENS	VESUVIUS
ERUPT	PLUME	VULCANOLOGIST
ETNA	POMPEII	

24. A REAL WORK OF ART

Each item in this word list contains the letters A-R-T in consecutive order. When these letters appear in the grid, they have been replaced by a □ . So, for example, SLUMBER PARTY would appear as SLUMBERP□Y. The grid, by the way, is shaped like a framed painting—in other words, a work of art. The hidden message is a five-word sentence that contains four more "words of art."

```
K  I  N  D  E  R  G  □  E  N  M  □  E
L  I                             L  □
A     C  □  Y  F  □  H  E  S  T     P
T     O  K  W  A  L  M  □  T  Q     A
□     U  O  S  S  T  W  I  N  U     N
E     R  G  □  T  G  L  N  A  □     O
H     T  U  S  O  □  A  D  P  E     B
O     M  A  H  U  M  M  □  Y  R     N
T     □  N  T  □  □  D  E  □  B     O
□     I  S  C  S  G  E  D  M  A     E
E     A  P  □  M  E  N  T  S  C     L
H     L  T  P  E  L  C  I  □  K     O
□     P  I  E  C  H  □  M  K  E     P
N  O                             T  A
P  □  L  Y  B  □  S  I  M  P  S  O  N
```

APARTMENTS	HEART-TO-HEART TALK	PARTLY
ARTICLE	HOGWARTS	PIE CHART
BART SIMPSON	KICK-START	POP TARTS
CARTMAN	KINDERGARTEN	QUARTERBACK
COURT-MARTIAL	KING ARTHUR	SMARTY-PANTS
DARTED	MARTYR	STUART LITTLE
FARTHEST	NAPOLEON BONAPARTE	WAL-MART
GO-KART		

25. ON THE FACE OF IT

Shaped like a face tilted very slightly towards us, this grid contains things you might put on your face. The hidden message is a sassy insult by old-time movie comedian Groucho Marx that begins, "I never forget a face, but …"

```
        I  S  O  A  P  N
     C  I  C  E  P  A  C  K  Y
  O  R  U  K  S  M  R  O  F  C  H
  A  E  S  S  S  O  E  O  A  N  T
  B  A  N  D  A  I  D  T  C  E  O
  M  M  M  I  L  S  L  T  E  E  L  L
  M  L  A  A  G  T  E  A  P  R  C  K
  F  A  K  E  M  U  S  T  A  C  H  E
  E  B  E  A  R  R  O  N  I  S  S
  E  P  U  X  E  I  N  L  N  N  A
  E  I  P  T  D  Z  N  O  T  U  W
     L  A  C  W  E  W  T  O  S
     W  I  E  O  R  O  I  P
        T  M  P  I  L  O  O
        N  S  S  C  N
```

BAND-AID	LIP BALM	SMILE
CLOWN NOSE	LOTION	SOAP
CREAM	MAKEUP	SUNSCREEN
FACE PAINT	MASK	TATTOO
FAKE MUSTACHE	MOISTURIZER	WASHCLOTH
GLASSES	OILS	WATER
ICE PACK	POWDER	

26. "DO YOU READ ME?"

So how's your solving going so far? Has it been fun? Challenging? Way too easy? Just right? Do you find that the words going across and straight down are simple to see but the words going backwards or at a slant are trickier to spot? Do you like the grids that have a picture shape like the penguin or the volcano or the vase, or is the plain rectangle fine for you? How about the rebuses? Those little pictures that represent a sequence of letters can strain your brain — but hopefully in a playful way. As for hidden messages, not being neat when you circle words in the grid can lead to confusion, as you may have learned. Of course, figuring out how to divide the string of leftover letters into words and sentences can be a tough task, but we trust the payoff is worth the effort. Speaking of effort, it's now time for you to come up with the word list for the puzzle below. All 24 words hidden in the grid can be found in the paragraph you're now reading. (Hah! And you thought we were just shooting the breeze!) So pick up your pencil again and see how much you can read into what you've just read.

HINTS:

1) None of the hidden words are in these hints.

2) To make solving easier, we've made all the leftover letters X's, so no X's will appear in hidden words and there will be no hidden message, just 26 X's. That means that all of the other letters in the grid will be used.

3) There are no hidden phrases, just hidden words. Each word will be at least four letters long. Only five words are on diagonals.

4) If you need it, the complete word list can be found on page 66.

```
X  B  A  C  K  W  A  R  D  S  X
X  B  S  H  A  P  E  R  R  V  X
V  R  T  A  S  K  B  E  L  O  W
X  A  X  L  X  X  C  I  E  L  Y
X  I  S  L  X  T  J  K  F  C  L
R  N  X  E  A  X  U  C  F  A  L
E  C  O  N  F  U  S  I  O  N  U
P  P  G  G  X  F  T  R  R  O  F
R  L  L  I  K  E  O  T  T  P  E
E  A  X  N  X  S  X  Y  E  X  P
S  Y  X  G  X  X  T  N  A  X  O
E  F  P  A  R  A  G  R  A  P  H
N  U  E  S  R  U  O  C  I  X  X
T  L  X  S  I  M  P  L  E  N  X
X  S  E  N  T  E  N  C  E  S  G
```

27. KEY CHAIN

This grid contains the names of keys and symbols on a standard computer keyboard. If you do normal touch typing, there are just two U.S. states that you can type using only one hand. The hidden message names those states and the hand you use.

```
H  S  A  L  S  K  C  A  B  T  H
E  L  P  E  R  I  O  D  A  S  H
R  A  T  F  I  H  S  C  I  R  Y
Q  U  O  T  E  S  O  G  H  I  P
U  Q  P  P  N  N  N  T  K  G  H
E  E  T  A  T  G  G  S  F  H  E
S  T  I  R  O  R  I  O  H  T  N
T  E  O  E  I  R  S  S  E  B  O
I  L  N  N  E  O  R  R  T  R  L
O  E  A  T  D  N  A  D  T  A  O
N  D  S  H  L  C  L  H  M  C  C
M  A  E  E  I  L  L  M  E  K  F
A  P  O  S  T  R  O  P  H  E  T
R  F  O  I  R  C  D  T  E  T  X
K  A  S  S  P  A  C  E  B  A  R
```

APOSTROPHE	DASH	PERIOD
ASTERISK	DELETE	QUESTION MARK
AT SIGN	DOLLAR SIGN	QUOTES
BACKSLASH	EQUALS	RIGHT BRACKET
CARET	HYPHEN	SHIFT
COLON	LEFT PARENTHESIS	SPACE BAR
COMMA	OPTION	TILDE
CONTROL		

28. ON THE SUBWAY

This grid contains words associated with a subway. The hidden message names the cities that have the most subway riders, starting with the fourth-most and proceeding in order to the topmost, which may surprise you.

```
E  X  P  R  E  S  S  U  N  L  C
E  P  W  L  Y  O  P  E  I  R  O
N  O  I  T  A  T  S  A  A  Y  N
K  L  C  I  O  T  R  C  A  T  D
E  E  O  W  E  D  F  L  T  I  U
L  N  N  C  R  Y  E  O  S  X  C
I  N  E  I  A  D  O  S  R  E  T
T  U  H  U  F  L  L  I  M  M  O
S  T  R  A  P  H  A  N  G  E  R
N  W  A  I  T  I  N  G  O  S  R
R  S  C  O  W  A  R  D  T  N  I
U  N  D  E  R  G  R  O  U  N  D
T  R  A  I  N  D  P  O  U  T  E
T  R  A  N  S  F  E  R  O  T  K
Y  O  R  U  O  H  H  S  U  R  E
```

CLOSING DOORS	POLE	THIRD RAIL
CONDUCTOR	RIDE	TRAIN
DELAY	ROUTE	TRANSFER
EXIT	RUSH HOUR	TUNNEL
EXPRESS	SEAT	TURNSTILE
FARE	STATION	UNDERGROUND
LOCAL	STOP	UPTOWN
PLATFORM	STRAPHANGER	WAITING

29. SAME AND DIFFERENT

Shaped like a chocolate kiss, this grid contains words that are spelled the same but have very different meanings. To find out what those grid words are, use the clues on the opposite page. Each clue gives you two definitions for each word, and the blanks tell you the number of letters in each word. As an added hint, the missing words from 1 to 20 are in alphabetical order. Work back and forth between the words you can define and words you discover in the grid. The hidden message spells out two more clues for the same word. Can you figure out what that extra word is?

(If you need help, the complete word list can be found on page 67.)

CLUES

1. Square-jawed dog, and an athlete who competes in a ring   _ _ _ _ _

2. London or Sacramento, and an uppercase letter   _ _ _ _ _ _ _

3. Train worker, and an orchestra leader   _ _ _ _ _ _ _ _ _

4. Nashville music, and China or Chile   _ _ _ _ _ _ _

5. Judge's workplace, and where a tennis match takes place   _ _ _ _ _

6. A split in the sidewalk, and a sassy remark   _ _ _ _ _

7. Group habits, and taxes paid at international airports   _ _ _ _ _ _ _

8. Business venture, and a *Star Trek* ship   _ _ _ _ _ _ _ _ _ _

9. What a soccer player kicks with, and twelve inches   _ _ _ _

10. New Year's Eve thing to blow, and a rhino feature   _ _ _ _

11. Brightly colored flower, and an eye part   _ _ _ _

12. What you type on at a computer, and what you use to play a piano or organ _ _ _ _ _ _ _ _

13. Chocolate treat (the shape of this puzzle grid), and a smooch   _ _ _ _

14. Device to secure a suitcase, and a canal section   _ _ _ _

15. School hall watcher, and a computer screen   _ _ _ _ _ _ _

16. The time right now, and a birthday gift   _ _ _ _ _ _ _

17. Housing for military personnel, and U.S. coins   _ _ _ _ _ _ _ _

18. Overthrow of a government, and a full cycle of our planet around the sun   _ _ _ _ _ _ _ _ _ _

19. One who reigns, and a straightedge   _ _ _ _ _

20. Car storage area, and an elephant's picker-upper   _ _ _ _ _

30. STAMP OF APPROVAL

This stamp-shaped grid contains words and images that appeared on U.S. 39-cent stamps in 2007. The first two U.S. stamps were introduced at the same time in 1847. The five-cent stamp featured Benjamin Franklin, America's first postmaster general, who also shows up on our list below. The hidden message tells about that other famous first stamp.

```
T   H   H   E   B   T   E
  J   E   W   E   L   R   Y   N   E   C   E
L   U   N   A   R   N   E   W   Y   E   A   R   N
  L   T   O   S   R   E   D   N   O   W   N
T   R   A   E   H   E   L   P   R   U   P   N   S
  E   E   D   E   H   A   N   R   O   C   H
H   A   P   P   Y   B   I   R   T   H   D   A   Y
  G   E   D   S   L   Q   C   B   G   A   N
E   A   L   O   K   U   I   I   R   Z   M   U   G
  N   L   N   I   E   R   B   N   F   E   K
W   A   A   L   S   D   A   A   E   S   L   K   H
  R   T   K   S   T   W   R   I   R   O   A
F   S   I   N   M   K   G   A   T   O   T   H   G
  E   K   A   L   F   W   O   N   S   T   Y
R   N   N   O   N   I   T
```

ARABIC	HANUKKAH	PURPLE HEART
BATMAN	HAPPY BIRTHDAY	QUILTS
BEANS	HERSHEY'S KISS	[RONALD] REAGAN
[BLUE] BIRDS	[NAVAJO] JEWELRY	SKIER
CORN	KWANZAA	SNOWFLAKE
ELLA [FITZGERALD]	LADY LIBERTY	WONDERS [OF
FLAG	LUNAR NEW YEAR	AMERICA]
[BEN] FRANKLIN	MEL OTT	

31. WEAR IT PROUDLY

Shaped like the vase on the merit badge for pottery, this grid contains the names of 20 activities for which one can earn a merit badge in the Boy Scouts of America. (There are more than 120 merit badge activities in all.) The hidden message names three more such badges, all of which are very different from each other.

```
            M U S I C
      R R       R H O       F I
  F       A   L W O I E   A       S
  H         D A K O W K M         O
    B U G L I N G N I I K S T
        Y N F O I L N N
        N G L A G Y N D T G G
        H O N V L E A I A T E
        G L F I R S T A I D R
        A O F A D N U N D W E
          E E T P A R L A N
          G T I E H E O E E
            P O T T E R Y
            N S R G E
            R Y A
```

ART	GEOLOGY	PETS
AVIATION	GOLF	POTTERY
BUGLING	HIKING	RADIO
COOKING	INDIAN LORE	READING
ENERGY	LAW	ROWING
FAMILY LIFE	MUSIC	[WATER] SKIING
FIRST AID	NATURE	

32. THE NEW WORLD

This grid contains 22 countries found in the Western Hemisphere. Four more New World nations are located in the hidden message.

```
J  C  O  L  O  M  B  I  A  E  C
A  N  A  Y  U  G  E  L  S  U  H
M  A  D  A  N  A  C  X  B  N  I
A  B  O  L  I  V  I  A  I  I  L
I  A  L  I  T  I  A  H  V  C  E
C  V  E  N  E  Z  U  E  L  A  O
A  O  A  D  D  O  R  E  B  R  Y
N  A  S  R  S  B  C  A  D  A  A
I  L  O  T  T  U  S  U  G  U  U
T  I  A  L  A  M  E  T  A  U  G
N  Z  R  D  T  R  I  N  A  A  A
E  A  O  B  E  L  I  Z  E  P  R
G  R  M  E  S  P  A  C  E  N  A
R  B  H  O  N  D  U  R  A  S  P
A  A  Y  A  U  G  U  R  U  M  A
```

ARGENTINA	CUBA	MEXICO
BELIZE	ECUADOR	NICARAGUA
BOLIVIA	GUATEMALA	PARAGUAY
BRAZIL	GUYANA	PERU
CANADA	HAITI	UNITED STATES
CHILE	HONDURAS	URUGUAY
COLOMBIA	JAMAICA	VENEZUELA
COSTA RICA		

33. WORDPLAY

All the words and phrases in this puzzle have to do with Scrabble. The hidden message answers this riddle: Why are Scrabble players like a lot of comedians?

```
T C E N N O C B E K W
R C X A U R S E C T A
I H C E Y E U A S B R
P P H O N Y R T T O D
L P A S S T B O U I R
E G N E L L A H C H E
T L G G A B I T K S V
R K E N P L I E W L O
I T K I O O T P I E L
P S A D N C I Y T W R
L W D A I K L N H O E
E S R E T T E L T V M
M Y A L T H S W H S I
A T O U R N A M E N T
G O B O N U S R Q D S
```

BLANKS	GAME	SCORE
BLOCK	LEADING	STUCK WITH THE Q
BOARD	LETTERS	TILES
BONUS	OVERDRAW	TIMER
CHALLENGE	PASS	TOURNAMENT
CONNECT	PHONY	TRIPLE-TRIPLE
DICTIONARY	POINTS	TURN
EXCHANGE	RACK	VOWELS

34. HOLIDAY HIGHLIGHTS

This dreidel-shaped grid contains words and phrases associated with holidays celebrated in the United States. (A dreidel is a top that's spun for fun during Hanukkah.) The hidden message answers this riddle: What do you call the time when strings of Christmas tree bulbs are on sale?

```
                  J
                  A
                  C
                  K
    H  G  S  K  R  O  W  E  R  I  F
    O  O  U  L  I  L  G  P  L  D  A
    I  H  A  V  E  A  D  R  E  A  M
    E  D  L  S  L  N  Y  E  P  P  S
    D  N  C  F  H  T  L  S  R  O  S
    A  U  I  I  L  E  D  I  E  R  D
    R  O  G  T  H  R  S  D  C  D  R
    A  R  B  U  N  N  Y  E  H  L  A
    P  G  T  R  O  E  S  N  A  L  C
    A  V  I  K  Z  N  L  T  U  A  G
       T  R  E  T  O  V  A  N  B
       I  Y  A  S  T  E  V
          M  M  E
```

ASHES	FLAG	PRESIDENT
BALL DROP	GROUNDHOG	SALE
BUNNY	"I HAVE A DREAM…"	TURKEY
CARDS	JACK O'LANTERN	VALENTINE
CLAUS	LEPRECHAUN	VETS
DREIDEL	MATZO	VOTER
FIREWORKS	PARADE	

35. TREE ENTRIES

This tree-shaped grid contains the names of 22 trees. The hidden message contains two more trees, each of which has a funny-sounding name.

```
        K A E T     M O P N
      S K O S E L P A M L T
    E Y Y L M O E R E B B U R
    H C R I B D M G A P O N M
      A L V D O O I A S N T
    D M G E O G N A M U P S M
  W O L L I W G N I P E E W
    B R O     O I T     A H N
      E L     O N S     R C
              D K E
              I G Q
              E O U
              M N O
              M L I
          A Y A P A P B
        O E U C A L Y P T U S
```

ASPEN	LIME	PEAR
BIRCH	MANGO	PINE
CHESTNUT	MAPLE	PLUM
DOGWOOD	MIMOSA	RUBBER
EUCALYPTUS	OLIVE	SYCAMORE
GIANT SEQUOIA	PALM	TEAK
GINKGO	PAPAYA	WEEPING WILLOW
LEMON		

36. CEREAL BOX

This grid contains the names of 20 popular breakfast cereals. General Mills puts out three "monster" cereals: Franken Berry and Count Chocula (which are in the grid) and Boo Berry (which is not). The company no longer puts out two other monster cereals. The hidden message names those cereals and the cartoon monsters on their boxes.

```
F  S  P  O  O  L  T  O  O  R  F
R  M  P  S  M  O  R  Z  F  C  M
A  R  R  E  U  I  L  A  T  O  T
N  A  T  K  C  B  R  X  O  U  M
K  H  U  A  T  I  E  B  E  N  O
E  C  A  L  P  H  A  B  I  T  S
N  Y  T  F  C  K  H  L  E  C  T
B  K  W  D  T  E  E  R  K  H  U
E  C  H  E  E  R  I  O  S  O  N
R  U  E  T  W  H  I  O  L  C  E
R  L  F  S  A  S  N  X  D  U  P
Y  E  N  O  H  N  T  U  N  L  A
Y  N  A  R  B  N  I  S  I  A  R
U  M  M  F  Y  M  U  F  M  M  G
Y  S  K  C  A  J  E  L  P  P  A
```

ALPHA-BITS	FROSTED FLAKES	RAISIN BRAN
APPLE JACKS	GRAPE-NUTS	SHREK
CHEERIOS	KABOOM	SMORZ
CHEX	LIFE	SPECIAL K
COUNT CHOCULA	LUCKY CHARMS	TOTAL
FRANKEN BERRY	MOST	TRIX
FROOT LOOPS	NUT 'N HONEY	

37. PLAY PEN

Each item in this word list contains the letters P-E-N in consecutive order. When these letters appear in the grid, they have been replaced by a ✎. So, for example, INDEPENDENCE DAY would appear as INDE✎DENCEDAY. Now S✎D a few moments looking at the list. The hidden message contains a few more ✎s and completes this sentence: Because he started a fight during the game, the hockey player was …

```
S   R   U   C   A   ✎   T   E   R   ✎
✎   A   N   D   ✎   C   I   L   S   E   T
✎   L   L   U   B   S   C   ✎   D   ✎   A
E   U   H   A   P   ✎   I   N   G   R   G
J   C   ✎   N   E   Y   L   D   N   A   O
A   I   N   G   D   ✎   L   C   I   H   N
T   D   E   A   I   A   I   O   D   S   L
I   ✎   S   Y   P   P   N   ✎   ✎   L   ✎
O   R   E   ✎   E   Z   E   H   S   I   I
✎   E   R   R   E   O   X   A   T   C   N
A   P   ✎   D   I   X   ✎   G   U   ✎   S
L   ✎   T   H   O   U   S   E   O   D   U
A   A   ✎   ✎   G   U   I   N   R   N   L
J   ✎   N   S   Y   L   V   A   N   I   A
Y   T   H   A   T   D   E   ✎   D   S   S
```

APPENDIX	JC PENNEY	PENNSYLVANIA
BULLPEN	OUTSPENDING	PENTAGON
CARPENTER	PEN AND PENCIL SET	PENTHOUSE
COPENHAGEN	PEN PAL	PERPENDICULAR
EYE OPENER	PENCIL SHARPENER	PIGPEN
HAPPENING	PENGUIN	REPENT
INEXPENSIVE	PENICILLIN	SERPENT
JALAPENO	PENINSULAS	"THAT DEPENDS…"

38. NOW BOARDING

This grid contains the names of airlines from around the world. The hidden message tells about the funny-named Turtle Airways. This small operation flies seaplanes in the beautiful and faraway South Pacific …

```
A  B  E  R  S  T  W  E  E  C  S
E  F  R  O  N  T  I  E  R  I  U
R  N  N  Y  V  T  M  U  O  F  N
L  G  R  A  L  I  T  A  L  I  A
I  T  R  L  R  I  L  T  Y  C  I
N  I  E  A  R  I  S  O  M  A  R
G  S  T  I  L  A  O  L  P  P  E
U  E  P  R  Q  S  U  F  I  Y  B
S  S  A  M  A  N  T  O  C  A  I
C  U  B  A  N  A  H  R  N  H  S
D  N  O  R  T  H  W  E  S  T  N
L  A  N  O  A  T  E  A  D  A  N
E  A  A  C  S  F  S  R  Y  C  B
A  I  L  A  G  U  T  R  O  P  Y
F  I  J  E  U  L  B  T  E  J  I
```

AER LINGUS	JETBLUE	RYAN
AEROFLOT	LUFTHANSA	SIBERIA
ALITALIA	NORTHWEST	SONG
CATHAY PACIFIC	OLYMPIC	SOUTHWEST
CUBANA	PORTUGALIA	SPIRIT
EL AL	QANTAS	SUN AIR
EMIRATES	ROYAL AIR MAROC	VARIG
FRONTIER		

39. IN SHAPE

The words in this list are formed by taking and rearranging letters from a certain nine-letter word that contains no repeating letters. Each listed word contains from four to eight of those letters and also never repeats a letter. By logic, can you figure out what the nine-letter starter word is? If not, read the hidden message: It'll tell you both the word and the shape of the grid.

```
            T  L  L  H
         E  R  E  A  L  I  T  Y
      A  A  A  I  R  E  T  S  Y  H
   S  Y  R  I  A        L  R  T  S  I
   L  S  T  L           A  E  I  S
   I  H  H              Y  L  H
   T  I  L              L  E  A
   H  R  Y              I  R  R
   E  T  H              S  E  E
   R  R  S              A  H  S
   Y  A  A              E  T  T
   L  E  R  S           L  I  A  S
      H  T  R        R  A  L
   S  A  T           Y  E  L
   Y  E              S  H
```

ALERT	LAYER	SHIRT
EARTHLY	LIST	SLITHER
EASILY	LYRE	STAY
HEAL	RAIL	STIR
HEART	REALITY	SYRIA
HITS	RELISH	TALES
HYSTERIA	REST	TRASHY
ISRAEL	SAIL	TRAY
LATHER	SHARE	

40. HEADS OR TAILS

This fun but tricky puzzle has several gimmicks. Both in the grid and in the word list, the words are connected from head to tail in a specific order to create one long chain of words. This means that the letter that ends the first word is exactly the same letter that begins the second word; the last letter in the second word is the exact letter that begins the third word; and so on right on through all 24 items.

First, build the word list by using the clues on the opposite page. Blanks help you with the number of letters, and you're given the first and last letters in every case.

Next, circle the words in the grid, in order if you can. Begin with START, the first answer, located at the top of the grid. The next word will begin with the T at the end of START and will go in some direction. In most cases the clue will suggest which way to proceed. For example, the second clue, "Falling down head over heels", suggests going down, and that is indeed the direction answer #2 goes in the grid. When you're finished, the circled words will form one long overlapping chain.

If this puzzle is twisting your brain too much, you can turn to page 67 for the complete word list. The hidden message is what you and other successful solvers might say after you've found your way around the grid.

```
S  T  A  R  T  O  T  D  N  E  L
D  E  T  O  U  R  E  D  N  O  P
O  S  T  T  M  P  E  O  O  U  E
O  P  O  S  B  L  D  W  G  E  R
T  F  K  H  L  G  O  N  A  R  I
S  E  O  T  I  U  I  W  E  N  M
W  L  D  R  N  O  I  A  N  T  E
E  L  A  O  G  C  I  R  R  H  T
N  C  L  N  E  Z  O  D  E  G  E
T  F  E  L  O  T  T  H  G  I  R
A  I  S  N  O  G  E  D  G  E  T
L  I  L  N  A  R  A  P  E  C  T
O  A  N  T  G  L  E  I  O  L  I
N  K  E  U  S  I  D  E  D  L  S
G  L  I  D  E  A  C  R  O  S  S
```

1. Begin   S _ _ _ T

2. Falling down head over heels, or doing acrobatics   T _ _ _ _ _ _ G

3. On the rise   G _ _ _ _   _ P

4. Outer border of a rectangle   P _ _ _ _ _ _ _ R

5. Direction you read Hebrew   R _ _ _ _   _ _   _ _ _ T

6. Slants off-center   T _ _ _ S

7. With "with," took the same position as someone in an argument

   S _ _ _ D

8. Slanting lines, not horizontals or verticals   D _ _ _ _ _ _ _ S

9. Arose from a chair   S _ _ _ D

10. Took an alternative route because the main one was closed

    D _ _ _ _ _ _ D

11. Toward the ground   D _ _ _ _ _ _ D

12. A group of the number of this clue, like eggs   D _ _ _ N

13. Opposite of south's   N _ _ _ _ ' S

14. Slant or distort   S _ _ W

15. Came with, or didn't disagree   W _ _ _   _ _ _ _ G

16. Skate effortlessly over the ice   G _ _ _ _   _ _ _ _ _ S

17. Slant on a ski mountain   S _ _ _ E

18. Outermost border, or what this answer in the grid is headed

    towards   E _ _ E

19. Number of the clue beginning with "Slanting lines"   E _ _ _ T

20. Incline, or look after a baby   T _ _ D

21. Over and finished, like you nearly are with this puzzle   D _ _ E

22. Words that finish this phrase that means "cause to stop": Put an

    E _ _   _ O

23. Having none left   O _ _   _ F

24. Tripped and hit the ground   F _ _ L

41. IN A FIX

This grid contains things you fix or that get fixed. The hidden message is an old saying about trying to change things when they're already perfectly fine.

```
K C A R C O N T E S T
P A P E R J A M C I N
T F I T O T I A A I O
E Y E S O T P I R C S
C B R O K E N B O N E
U N T P E C I R P M S
A S B F D R H O E B S
F A U L T Y V A L V E
Y N K A E E L A I P R
K D G T E D M O O R D
A W A T T E N T I O N
E I Z I H S H N N B R
L C E R T O T F E L O
I H X E L A I R T E T
I T P E K A T S I M D
```

[YOUR] ATTENTION
[THE] BLAME
BROKEN BONE
CONTEST
CRACK
CROOKED TEETH
[YOUR] EYES [ON SOMETHING]
FAULTY VALVE
FLAT TIRE
[YOUR] GAZE

[YOUR] HAIR
LEAKY FAUCET
MEAL
MISTAKE
NEED
[YOUR] NOSE
PAPER JAM
PETS
[A] POSTER [TO A WALL]

POTHOLE
PRICE
PROBLEM
RACE
SANDWICH
SCRIPT
[A] TIME [TO DO SOMETHING]
TORN DRESS
TRIAL

42. WASHED UP

Shaped like a washing machine with a box of detergent on top, this grid contains things you wash and clean. The hidden message defines "nonsense" (which you'll find in a dictionary) or "a heap of laundry for a pig" (which we made up)!

```
            A  P  S
            P  N  E
            E  A  S
   P  O  T  S  I  N  C  K  N  I  S
   G  A  L  R  I  A  H  E  E  T  O
   O  F  N  L  R  D  W  A  L  L  S
   L  L  D  S  S  W  E  A  T  E  R
   F  E  I  H        W  C  O  S
   B  T  S           A  G  O
   A  T  H           T  L  C
   L  U  E           N  W  K
   L  C  S  D        E  O  A  S
   S  E  Y  R  E  N  I  H  C  A  M
   U  N  D  E  R  W  E  A  R  A  S
   G  L  A  S  S  R  E  T  L  I  F
   H  F  I  S  H  F  I  L  L  E  T
```

BED LINENS	GLASS	POTS
CARS	GOLF BALLS	SIDEWALK
CONTACT LENSES	HAIR	SINK
DISHES	LETTUCE	SOCKS
DRESS	MACHINERY	SWEATER
FACE	PANS	UNDERWEAR
FILTERS	PANTS	WALLS
FISH FILLET		

43. SPACESHIP EARTH

This rocket-shaped grid contains the names of some of the images and sounds that were sent on the Voyager 1 and 2 spacecraft in the 1970's as a message to any aliens who might encounter them, so as to give an idea of the variety of life and culture on Earth. The hidden message in the grid names one more image that was part of the message sent by NASA into space.

```
                S
              A E H
              U Q S
            L A U T O
            I R O A T
            F E I J E
            T D A M K
            O N I A R
            F U M H A
            F H S A M
            A T P L R
            B N E S E
            I A T A P
          L R H S W U E
        O T D P T I S N E
      I H N S E O N B S R C
    V A I   B L O G Y   I A H
    T W B   I E F R T   F K H
```

AUTO	KISS	SUPERMARKET
BIRDS	LIFT-OFF	SURF
EARTH	RAIN	TAJ MAHAL
ELEPHANT	SAWING	THUNDER
FIRE	SEQUOIA	VIOLIN
FOOTSTEPS	SPEECH	WIND

44. WITCHCRAFT

Shaped like a witch's head in profile, this grid contains words and phrases associated with witches. The hidden message is a tongue twister. Can you say it three times quickly?

BLACK MAGIC	COVEN	POTION
BREW	CURSE	SALEM
BROOMSTICK	DEVIL	THE WIZARD OF OZ
CACKLE	HANSEL	TOAD
CAST A SPELL	NARNIA	WART
CAULDRON	OWL	WICKED
CHARM	POINTY HAT	

45. WINDOW BOX

This grid contains words and phrases associated with windows. The hidden message completes this fun fact: The modern-day word "window" replaced two words from Old English. One word literally meant ...

```
S  L  E  N  A  P  G  E  Y  R  N
C  U  R  T  A  I  N  S  T  E  G
R  E  H  N  G  O  I  O  P  N  N
E  L  E  F  E  N  L  O  H  A  I
E  S  Y  R  T  S  I  K  S  E  P
N  S  T  A  E  S  E  N  A  L  P
S  H  R  M  S  A  C  A  W  C  O
H  U  I  E  M  L  O  R  E  A  H
O  T  D  T  A  G  T  C  H  E  S
H  T  F  O  S  O  R  C  I  M  E
S  E  D  A  H  S  O  R  W  E  L
A  R  G  Y  C  L  O  S  E  D  D
S  S  S  D  N  I  L  B  I  E  N
A  R  C  H  E  D  F  I  V  D  A
O  O  R  O  L  L  U  P  S  R  H
```

ARCHED	GLASS	SCREENS
AWNING	HANDLES	SHADES
BLINDS	LEDGE	SHUTTERS
CLEANER	MICROSOFT	SILL
CLOSED	OPEN	SMASH
CRANK	PANELS	TIME SLOT
CURTAINS	PANES	VIEW
DIRTY	PLANE SEAT	WASH
FLOOR-TO-CEILING	ROLL-UP	SHOPPING
FRAME	SASH	

46. "WATCH IT!"

This grid contains things you watch. The hidden message is one of the many famous quotes by baseball great Yogi Berra.

```
G  Y  M  A  N  N  E  R  S  F  O
N  B  A  B  Y  P  E  O  P  L  E
I  U  C  A  B  N  H  T  U  O  M
T  O  N  E  O  F  V  O  I  C  E
O  N  T  S  G  W  B  A  C  K  O
O  B  I  R  D  I  E  I  V  O  M
F  R  M  B  L  S  M  I  E  F  R
P  V  E  E  R  H  A  A  G  S  L
E  U  G  N  O  T  G  O  T  H  H
N  J  U  U  W  T  L  S  W  E  T
N  T  S  T  E  P  L  B  O  E  A
I  E  Y  I  H  W  A  A  H  P  E
E  T  D  C  T  H  B  I  S  N  R
S  E  L  B  A  U  L  A  V  G  B
T  E  N  N  I  S  M  A  T  C  H
```

[THE] BABY	[YOUR] MANNERS	THE WORLD GO BY
[YOUR] BACK	[YOUR] MOUTH	[THE] TIME
BALL GAME	MOVIE	[YOUR] TONE OF
[THE] BIRDIE	[YOUR] PENNIES	VOICE
[YOUR] BREATH	PEOPLE	[YOUR] TONGUE
[YOUR] DIET	PRISONER	TV SHOW
FLOCK OF SHEEP	[YOUR] STEP	[YOUR] VALUABLES
[YOUR] FOOTING	TENNIS MATCH	[YOUR] WEIGHT
[THE] HOUSE		

47. HIGH-GRADE FOOD

Every food on this list may not be high in vitamin A, but each item ends with the letter A. The grid is shaped liked a rutabaga, which is a vegetable. The hidden message answers this riddle: Why would it be easy for your whole class to do well on a spelling test of these foods?

```
            C  A  A
         U  A  N  A  N  A  B
      S  V  E  E  A  R  U  C  T
   Q  A  A  E  N  U  V  H  T  O  E
   U  R  V  G  G  C  A  Y  O  S  A
G  E  N  A  U  E  L  H  R  A  T  E  F
J  S  S  L  W  U  O  U  I  U  A  U  A
L  A  A  K  P  I  T  A  A  L  D  D  J
L  D  M  A  B  A  S  L  A  S  A  E  I
S  I  U  B  B  R  F  E  T  O  N  D  T
A  L  E  A  A  M  O  U  S  S  A  K  A
   L  G  N  D  L  A  Z  Z  I  P  U
   A  L  L  E  R  A  Z  Z  O  M  P
      W  I  K  I  T  Y  H  A  E
         O  T  A  T  S  A  P
            R  N  A
               O
               T
```

ARUGULA	FLAUTA	PITA
BAKLAVA	GUAVA	PIZZA
BANANA	JAMBALAYA	QUESADILLA
CHALUPA	LASAGNA	RUTABAGA
EMPANADA	MOUSSAKA	SALSA
ENCHILADA	MOZZARELLA	TORTILLA
FAJITA	OKRA	TOSTADA
FETA	PASTA	TUNA

48. FLAGS

Shaped like a Star of David, this grid lists the names of shapes and symbols found on various national flags from around the world. If you're curious about which countries' flags bear these symbols, turn to page 67. As for the hidden message . . . it tells you the only country that has a map of its country right on its national flag.

```
                        T
                    D   P   H
                    I   E   D
                L   V   R   D   I
    N   O   I   L   F   A   E   L   E   L   P   A   M
    S   Y   A   L   G   D   G   E   R   A   E   P   S
        R   I   O   A   F   G   I   L   D   N   T
            N   N   D   O   A   H   K   T   R
            C   N   A   Y   R   D   S   T   I   S   I
    I   O   R   N   O   A   U   F   P   C   S   A   B
    Y   N   O   O   M   T   N   E   C   S   E   R   C
                W   S   S   G   O
                    N   P   R
                    R   C   U
                        S
```

BIRD	DRAGON	SPEAR
CASTLE	LION	STAR OF DAVID
CRESCENT MOON	MAPLE LEAF	STRIPES
CROSS	PILLAR	TUSK
CROWN	SHIELD	YIN/YANG
DAGGER		

49. JUMPING FOR JOY

This grid contains words associated with gymnastics. The hidden message answers this riddle: If a famous hobbit was amazing in a certain men's gymnastics event, what should he be described as?

```
S  P  O  T  T  I  N  G  F  R  O
R  P  I  L  F  B  D  T  U  C  K
A  O  W  U  O  A  A  R  C  H  U
B  A  L  A  N  C  E  B  E  A  M
L  R  E  V  O  K  L  A  W  L  N
E  F  O  L  D  B  B  E  H  K  O
L  F  T  T  A  E  R  I  A  L  I
L  O  A  L  A  N  D  I  N  G  T
A  D  R  H  E  D  L  O  D  R  C
R  N  D  O  D  T  W  I  S  T  U
A  U  O  F  O  I  T  G  P  H  D
P  O  M  M  E  L  H  O  R  S  E
E  R  R  I  N  P  F  G  I  I  D
T  N  U  O  M  S  I  D  N  S  P
S  G  N  I  R  A  B  H  G  I  H
```

AERIAL	FLOOR	RINGS
ARCH	GRIP	ROUND-OFF
BACKBEND	HANDSPRING	SPLIT
BALANCE BEAM	HIGH BAR	SPOTTING
CHALK	LANDING	TUCK
DEDUCTION	LEOTARD	TWIST
DISMOUNT	PARALLEL BARS	VAULT
FLIP	POMMEL HORSE	WALKOVER

50. THAT'S FUNNY

Shaped like a speech balloon from the funny papers, this grid contains the names of comic strip characters. The hidden message tells what the King in "The Wizard of Id" thinks about the inhabitants of his kingdom.

```
        E  H  H  A  G  A  R  E
     L  N  A  M  R  E  H  T  R  E
  L  D  F  F  I  L  C  H  T  A  E  H
Y  I  I  A  M  M  O  M  C  A  T  H  Y  F
E  N  L  M  R  O  A  A  S  K  I  N  G  T
O  U  B  T  M  Z  N  G  H  Y  G  G  I  Z
T  S  E  N  R  E  D  N  A  K  N  A  R  F
  L  R  A  E  B  J  E  A  C  E  M  A
     T  S  I  R  A  S  D  U  O  I
        E  T  A  N  G  I  B  L
           I  E  M
        O  S  I
        T  O  J
     S  R
```

AGNES	FRANK AND ERNEST	LINUS
ARLO AND JANIS	GRIMM	LUANN
BIG NATE	HAGAR	MOMMA
BUCKY KATT	HEATHCLIFF	MOOCH
CATHY	HERMAN	ROSE
DILBERT	JIMBO	ZEBRA
EARL	[THE] KING	ZIGGY
ELLY		

51. CLOSING NOTICE

Shaped like a tombstone, this last grid quite appropriately contains words and phrases associated with the end of something. The hidden message tells you an easy way to make a friend.

```
              S  L  E  E  P
           A  P  A  S  C  N  T
        N  B  A  S  O  H  E  O  S
        B  E  T  T  O  E  W  M  I
     R  E  V  M  D  B  C  Y  B  G  P
     F  G  I  A  A  A  K  E  S  N  R
     I  I  T  E  Y  C  E  A  T  A  E
     N  V  N  F  O  F  R  R  O  T  S
     A  E  R  I  F  T  E  S  N  U  S
     L  U  M  O  S  I  D  E  E  R  C
     S  P  G  O  C  H  F  V  D  E  L
     A  O  Y  W  H  A  L  E  N  I  E
     L  D  X  A  O  O  A  I  A  D  A
     E  Y  B  D  O  O  G  T  N  D  R
     Z  E  N  D  L  B  U  Z  Z  E  R
```

AMEN	GO HOME	SLEEP
BUZZER	GOOD-BYE	SUNSET
CABOOSE	LAST DAY OF SCHOOL	TAIL
CHECKERED FLAG	LOG OFF	TAPS
FINALS	NEW YEAR'S EVE	TOMBSTONE
FINISH LINE	PRESS "CLEAR"	W,X,Y,Z
GIVE UP	SIGNATURE	

Answers

WORD LISTS

12. SIMPLY SUPER

1. SCREEN
2. SECOND
3. SERPENT
4. SERVICE
5. SHAKER
6. SHINE
7. SHOT
8. SHOVEL
9. SHUTTLE
10. SICK
11. SILVER
12. SIMON
13. SKIN
14. SLOPE
15. SONG
16. STACK
17. STAR
18. STORM
19. STORY
20. STROKE
21. SUDS
22. SUIT
23. SUPERINTENDENT
24. SYSTEM

21. TRIPLE PLAY

1. NATIONAL FOOTBALL LEAGUE
2. KENTUCKY FRIED CHICKEN
3. PARENT TEACHER ASSOCIATION
4. MOST VALUABLE PLAYER
5. CENTRAL INTELLIGENCE AGENCY
6. DIGITAL VIDEO DISC
7. UNIDENTIFIED FLYING OBJECT
8. WORLD WIDE WEB
9. VERY IMPORTANT PERSON
10. TENDER LOVING CARE
11. CABLE NEWS NETWORK
12. INTERNAL REVENUE SERVICE
13. AUTOMATED TELLER MACHINE

26. "DO YOU READ ME?"

BACKWARDS
BELOW
BRAIN
CHALLENGING
CONFUSION
COURSE
EFFORT
HOPEFULLY

JUST
LIKE
PARAGRAPH
PAYOFF
PENGUIN
PLAYFUL
RECTANGLE
REPRESENT

SENTENCES
SHAPE
SIMPLE
STRING
TASK
TRICKIER
VASE
VOLCANO

29. SAME AND DIFFERENT

1. BOXER
2. CAPITAL
3. CONDUCTOR
4. COUNTRY
5. COURT
6. CRACK
7. CUSTOMS
8. ENTERPRISE
9. FOOT
10. HORN
11. IRIS
12. KEYBOARD
13. KISS
14. LOCK
15. MONITOR
16. PRESENT
17. QUARTERS
18. REVOLUTION
19. RULER
20. TRUNK

40. HEADS OR TAILS

1. START
2. TUMBLING
3. GOING UP
4. PERIMETER
5. RIGHT TO LEFT
6. TILTS
7. SIDED
8. DIAGONALS
9. STOOD
10. DETOURED
11. DOWNWARD
12. DOZEN
13. NORTH'S
14. SKEW
15. WENT ALONG
16. GLIDE ACROSS
17. SLOPE
18. EDGE
19. EIGHT
20. TEND
21. DONE
22. END TO
23. OUT OF
24. FELL

48. FLAGS

We did not list every single instance where these shapes and symbols appear, so with research you may discover other national flags that bear these images.

BIRD – A yellow bird (Zimbabwe), an eagle (Egypt), a crested crane (Uganda)

CASTLE – Portugal, Spain

CRESCENT MOON – Turkey and several others

CROSS – Switzerland and several others

CROWN – Liechtenstein, Spain

DAGGER – Oman

DRAGON – Bhutan

LION – Sri Lanka, Spain

MAPLE LEAF – Canada

PILLAR – Spain

SHIELD – Kenya and others

SPEAR – Swaziland, Kenya

STAR OF DAVID – Israel

STRIPES – United States and many others

TUSK – A boar's tusk (Vanuatu)

YIN/YANG – South Korea

1. OPENING BELL

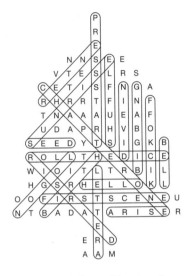

Never start a day without a dream.

2. COMING UP

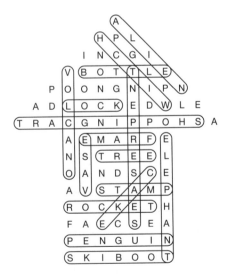

Ping-Pong paddle and a face.

3. BIRTH OF A NATION

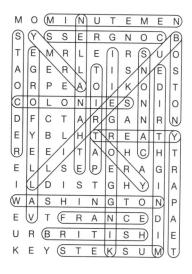

More respectable, he said, is the turkey.

4. TAKE YOUR PICK

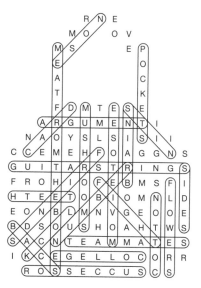

Remove tiny lice eggs from someone's hair.
(Lice eggs are called nits.)

5. THE PENGUIN

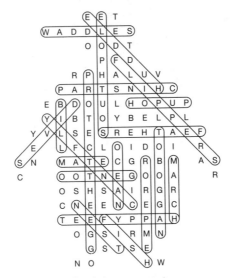

To travel by belly sliding across ice or snow.

6. PICK A NUMBER

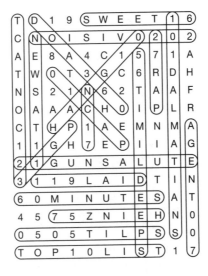

1984, Catch-22, Fahrenheit 451.

7. ALIEN INVASION

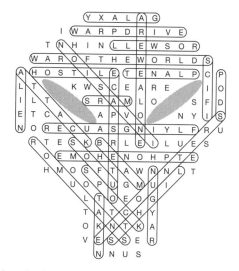

"I think we're lost. Can you tell us how to get to Venus?"

8. THIS IS *JEOPARDY!*

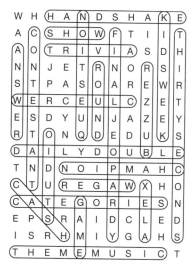

What is *Jeopardy!* (#2) and *The Price is Right?* (#1).

9. AUTO FOCUS

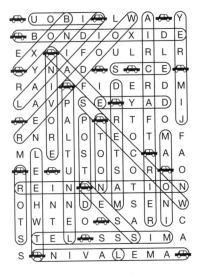

Carl carefully carried a carton of macaroons to Caracas.

10. POP CULTURE

A doctor named Charles T. Pepper. (Dr Pepper)

11. HITS POSSIBLE

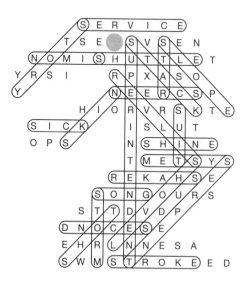

Played a hand-ball game against a chapel wall. (This is quite possibly how handball got started.)

12. SIMPLY SUPER

Seventy-six shortstops seesawed.

13. ISLE OF TWOPLAY
(Say it fast to get "I LOVE TO PLAY!")

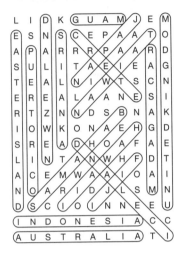

Like separate islands, none of the words connect. (Two bunches of diagonal words LOOK like their loops connect, but you'll notice they have no shared letters.)

14. LEWIS AND CLARK

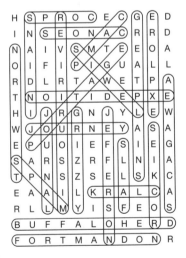

He did it a full ten years earlier. (Mackenzie was the first European to cross North America, including the Rocky Mountains and the Continental Divide, which he did in 1793.)

15. "CUT!"

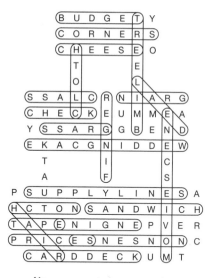

You may get a paper cut.

16. A HERD OF ANIMALS

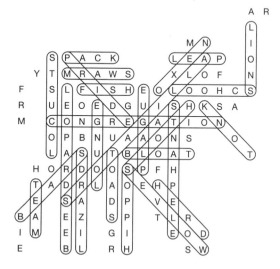

Army of frogs; ambush of tigers.

17. APT ANAGRAMS

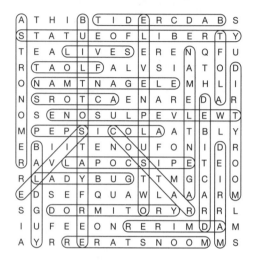

"This ear" equals "it hears." "Alien forms" equals "life on Mars."

18. AT THE SUPERMARKET

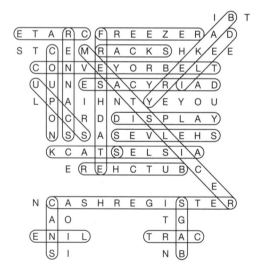

It's the line you're not in.

19. SNOW FUN

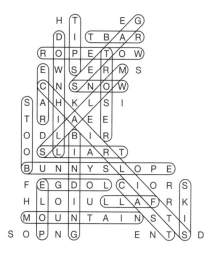

He skied for hours on end.

20. QUITE A COLLECTION

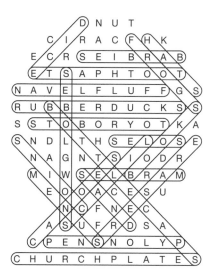

Nutcrackers and handcuffs.

21. TRIPLE PLAY

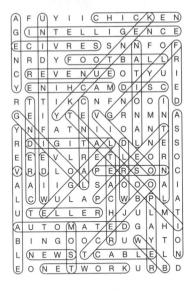

FYI is "for your information." LOL is "laughing out loud."

22. OUT TO SEA

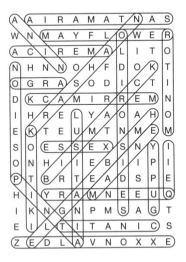

With no food, they ate their shipmates. (Yes, they resorted to cannibalism! Also, in case you wondered, the S.S. *Guppy* is the name of Cap'n Crunch's ship.)

23. VOLCANO!

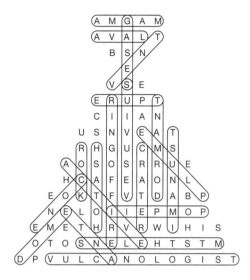

Because he blew his top.

24. A REAL WORK OF ART

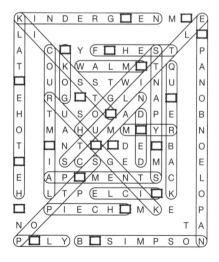

Marty starts an art department.

25. ON THE FACE OF IT

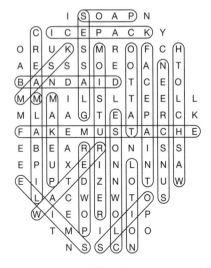

"… in your case, I'll make an exception."

26. "DO YOU READ ME?"

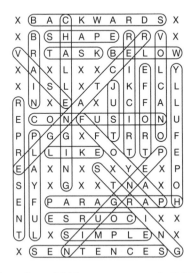

(There is no hidden message, only 26 X's.)

27. KEY CHAIN

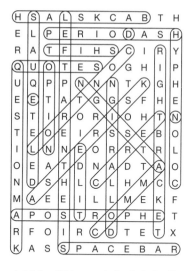

The right for Ohio, and the left for Texas.

28. ON THE SUBWAY

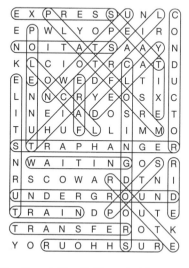

New York City, Seoul (South Korea), Moscow, and Tokyo.

29. SAME AND DIFFERENT

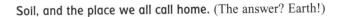

Soil, and the place we all call home. (The answer? Earth!)

30. STAMP OF APPROVAL

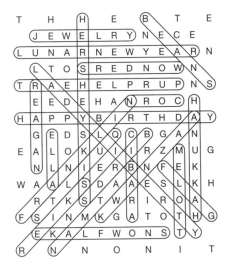

The ten-cent one had George Washington on it.

31. WEAR IT PROUDLY

Rifle shooting, theater, and weather.

32. THE NEW WORLD

El Salvador, Barbados, Suriname, Panama.

83

33. WORDPLAY

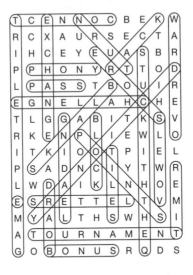

Because they both like to play with words.

34. HOLIDAY HIGHLIGHTS

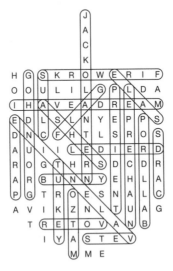

Holi-daylight saving time.

35. TREE ENTRIES

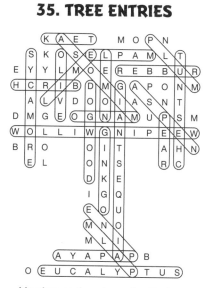

Monkeypod and gumbo-limbo.

36. CEREAL BOX

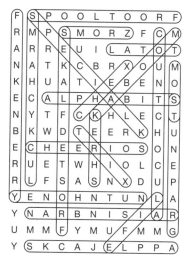

Fruit Brute (the werewolf) and Yummy Mummy.

37. PLAY PEN

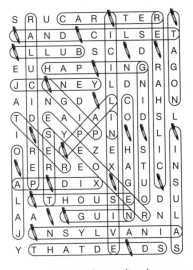

... suspended and penalized a penny.

38. NOW BOARDING

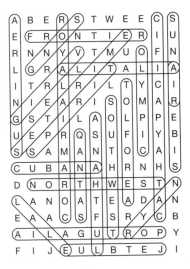

... between Turtle Island and nearby Fiji. (Turtle Island is a tiny private island for vacationers. Fiji is an independent island nation.)

39. IN SHAPE

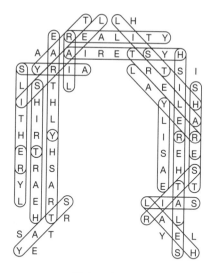

Hairstyle.

40. HEADS OR TAILS

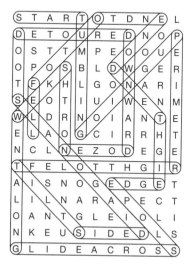

Lost people go around in circles, not in a rectangle like us.

41. IN A FIX

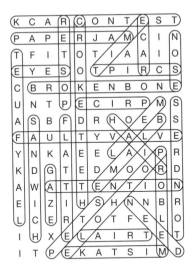

If it ain't broke, don't fix it.

42. WASHED UP

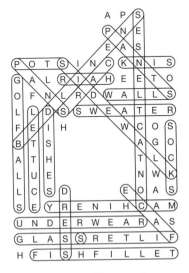

A pile of hogwash.

43. SPACESHIP EARTH

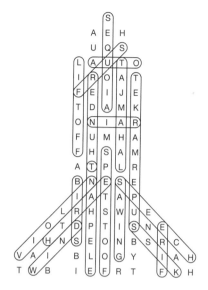

A human baby at birth.

44. WITCHCRAFT

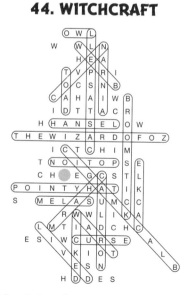

Which witch with itches switches wishes?

45. WINDOW BOX

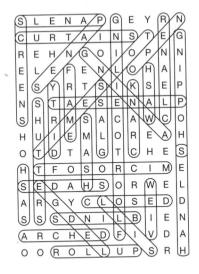

... eye-hole; the other, eye-door.

46. WATCH IT!

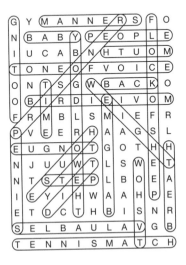

"You can observe a lot just by watching."

47. HIGH-GRADE FOOD

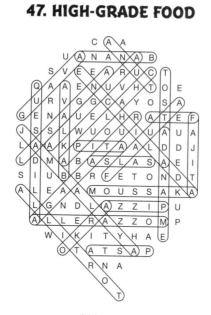

'Cause everyone would be sure to end up with an A.

48. FLAGS

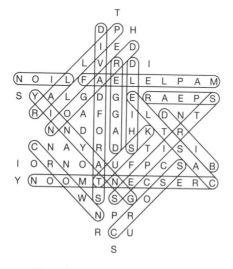

The island nation of Cyprus.

49. JUMPING FOR JOY

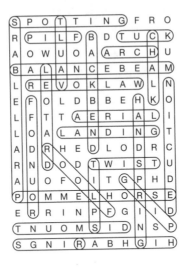

Frodo would be the lord of the rings.

50. THAT'S FUNNY

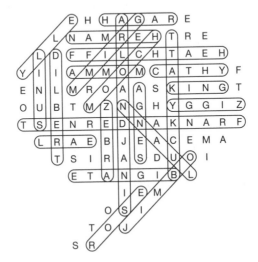

He refers to them as ld-iots.

51. CLOSING NOTICE

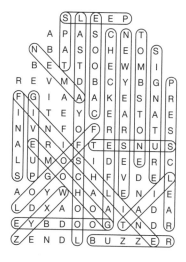

Abbreviate "Friday" and add "end." (Fri. + end = friend)

Index

Page key: puzzle, **word list**, *answers*.

About the Author

Mark Danna is a full-time puzzlemaker and a member of Mensa. Known for his playfulness, Danna writes the syndicated newspaper puzzle Wordy Gurdy, a page-a-day puzzle calendar for Mensa, and a wide range of puzzles for various clients. Danna was a longtime associate editor of *Games* magazine, a staff writer for a prime time TV game show, and a three-time National Frisbee Champion. He is now an avid tennis player, a talented swing dancer, and owner of more than 100 board games. *Challenging Word Search Puzzles for Kids* is his fourteenth word search book for Sterling.

WHAT IS MENSA?

Mensa®
The High IQ Society

Mensa is the international society for people with a high IQ. We have more than 100,000 members in over 40 countries worldwide.

The society's aims are:
- to identify and foster human intelligence for the benefit of humanity;
- to encourage research in the nature, characteristics, and uses of intelligence;
- to provide a stimulating intellectual and social environment for its members.

Anyone with an IQ score in the top two percent of the population is eligible to become a member of Mensa—are you the "one in 50" we've been looking for?

Mensa membership offers an excellent range of benefits:
- Networking and social activities nationally and around the world;
- Special Interest Groups (hundreds of chances to pursue your hobbies and interests—from art to zoology!);
- Monthly International Journal, national magazines, and regional newsletters;
- Local meetings—from game challenges to food and drink;
- National and international weekend gatherings and conferences;
- Intellectually stimulating lectures and seminars;
- Access to the worldwide SIGHT network for travelers and hosts.

For more information about Mensa International:
www.mensa.org
Telephone: +44 1400 272675
e-mail: enquiries@mensa.org
Mensa International Ltd.
Slate Barn
Church Lane
Caythorpe, Lincolnshire NG32 3EL
United Kingdom

For more information about American Mensa:
www.us.mensa.org
Telephone: 1-800-66-MENSA
American Mensa Ltd.
1229 Corporate Drive West
Arlington, TX 76006-6103 USA

For more information about British Mensa (UK and Ireland):
www.mensa.org.uk
Telephone: +44 (0) 1902 772771
e-mail: enquiries@mensa.org.uk
British Mensa Ltd.
St. John's House
St. John's Square
Wolverhampton WV2 4AH
United Kingdom

For more information about Australian Mensa:
www.mensa.org.au
Telephone: +61 1902 260 594
e-mail: info@mensa.org.au
Australian Mensa Inc.
PO Box 212
Darlington WA 6070 Australia